Canada's
LAND & PEOPLE

BRITISH COLUMBIA

Jill Foran

Weigl

CALGARY

www.weigl.com

Published by Weigl Educational Publishers Limited
6325 10 Street SE
Calgary, Alberta   T2H 2Z9

Website: www.weigl.com
Copyright ©2008 Weigl Educational Publishers Limited
All rights reserved. No part of this publication may be reproduced, stored in a retrieval system, or transmitted in any form or by any means, electronic, mechanical, photocopying, recording, or otherwise, without the prior written permission of Weigl Educational Publishers Limited.

Library and Archives Canada Cataloguing in Publication

Foran, Jill
        British Columbia / Jill Foran.

(Canada's land and people)
Includes index.
ISBN 978-1-55388-349-4 (bound)
ISBN 978-1-55388-350-0 (pbk.)

        1. British Columbia--Juvenile literature. I. Title. II. Series.
FC3811.2.F675 2007   j971.1   C2007-902208-1

Printed in the United States of America
1 2 3 4 5 6 7 8 9 0 11 10 09 08 07

We acknowledge the financial support of the Government of Canada through the Book Publishing Industry Development Program (BPIDP) for our publishing activities.

Photograph credits: Provincial Government of British Columbia: page 4 top.

Project Coordinator
Heather C. Hudak

Design
Terry Paulhus

ontents

About British Columbia

British Columbia is Canada's province farthest to the West. It is nicknamed "The Pacific Province" because it is the only province that borders the Pacific Ocean. British Columbia is the third-largest province in Canada, after Ontario and Quebec. It covers about 947,800 square kilometres of land.

British Columbia became a province on July 20, 1871. It was named by Great Britain's Queen Victoria. Its name refers to Great Britain and to the Columbia River, which flows through the province.

The official stone of British Columbia is jade. Jade is a mineral. It can be made into jewellery, sculptures, ornaments, tiles, and tabletops.

The official motto of British Columbia is *Splendor Sine Occasu*. This is Latin for "splendour without diminishment."

ABOUT THE FLAG

British Columbia's flag was adopted in 1960. It symbolizes British Columbia's past as a British colony and its landscape. The top half of the flag is Great Britain's **Union Jack** with a crown in the middle. The bottom half shows the Sun and wavy lines. These show the province's location between the Rocky Mountains and the Pacific Ocean. The flag's design comes from British Columbia's shield of arms.

LEGEND

N

Yukon
Northwest Territories
Nunavut
British Columbia
Alberta
Manitoba
Newfoundland & Labrador
Saskatchewan
Ontario
Quebec
Prince Edward Island
New Brunswick
Nova Scotia

ACTION Design your own flag for British Columbia. What colours and pictures would you include on your flag?

Places to Visit in British Columbia

There are many places to see in British Columbia. This map shows just a few. What places do you think are special in British Columbia? Can you find where they would be on the map?

CANADA

British Columbia has the longest railway tunnel in North America. It is called Mount Macdonald Tunnel. It runs for 14.7 kilometres. This tunnel is located in the Selkirk Mountains, in Glacier National Park.

Vernon is home to the Okanagan Opal deposit, where people can dig for opal. Opal is a mineral from which gemstone is made.

British Columbia's largest city is Vancouver.

...ctoria is the capital city of British ...olumbia. The government of British ...olumbia is in Victoria.

Juneau

Petersburg

Prince Rupert

British Columbia

Dawson Creek

Prince George

Glacier National Park

Kootenay National Park

Kamloops

Merritt

Vernon

Kelowna

Trail

Vancouver

Burnaby

Victoria

UNITED STATES

Everett

Spokane

SCALE
200 Miles
200 Kilometres
N

Beautiful Landscapes

British Columbia is known throughout the world for its natural beauty. Here, there are some of the oldest trees, highest mountains, and roughest rivers in North America. This province is one of the few places in the world to have warm beaches, snow-capped mountains, and a dry desert. While kayaking along the coastline, people can view the lush, peaceful islands. The rolling grasslands and moss-covered forests make for a pleasant afternoon hike.

On the eastern border of British Columbia are four mountain ranges. They are the Rocky Mountains, the Purcells, the Selkirks, and the Monashees. Together, they are called the British Columbia Rockies. On the western border of the province are the Coast Mountains. These stretch from the Yukon border, in the North, almost to the United States, in the South. Their height is more than 2,000 metres above sea level.

Fruit orchards and wineries grow in the Thompson Okanagan region. This is in the centre of the province, between rich farmlands and the Rocky Mountains.

The Gulf Islands are a chain of large and small islands where the province reaches the Pacific Ocean. In this quiet region, there are small communities that have craft markets and art studios.

In the centre of the province is Cariboo Country. It is between the Cariboo Mountain Range and the Pacific Ocean. Cariboo Country has rolling hills, deep rivers, and many lakes.

In the southern interior valley of the Thompson Okanagan region is a desert that is about 24 kilometres long. Summer temperatures can rise above 37 degrees Celsius. This region has plants and animals, such as prickly pear cacti and rattlesnakes.

Northern British Columbia is known for its large salmon and steelhead trout. During August and September, salmon swim upstream to Babine Lake to lay and fertilize their eggs.

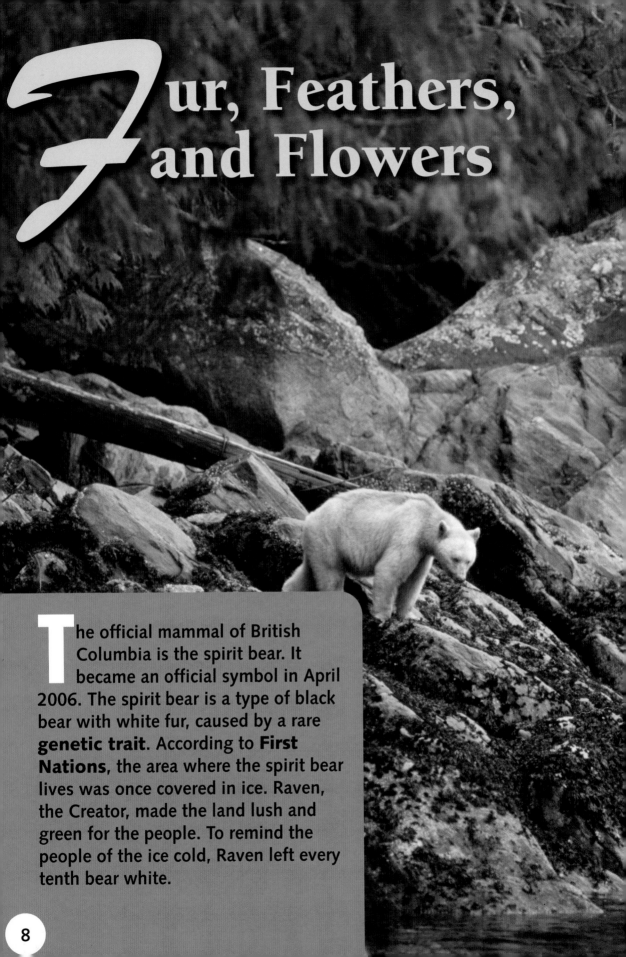

Fur, Feathers, and Flowers

The official mammal of British Columbia is the spirit bear. It became an official symbol in April 2006. The spirit bear is a type of black bear with white fur, caused by a rare **genetic trait**. According to **First Nations**, the area where the spirit bear lives was once covered in ice. Raven, the Creator, made the land lush and green for the people. To remind the people of the ice cold, Raven left every tenth bear white.

In 1987, children of British Columbia chose the Stellar's jay as the province's bird. This jay is found throughout the province. It is brightly coloured blue and black and is often mistaken for the blue jay.

The Pacific dogwood is British Columbia's floral emblem, or symbol. The Pacific dogwood is a flowering tree that grows 6 to 8 metres high. It has beautiful white flowers that open in the spring. In autumn, the Pacific dogwood has bright red berries.

The western red cedar is the province's official tree. These trees live in the moist, coastal regions of the province. They can grow as high as 60 metres.

On the mainland of British Columbia are many grizzly bears, porcupines, moose, skunks, and coyotes. Vancouver Island has the densest population of cougars in North America.

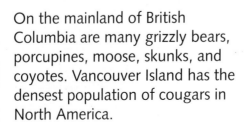

Rich in Resources

British Columbia is rich in natural resources. Its most important resource is its forests. Forests cover more than half of the province. These forests provide all of Canada with about half of its **softwood** needs. Cone-bearing trees, called conifers, are used to make lumber, newsprint, and other paper products. The land is also rich in metals and minerals. These are used to make many things, such as computer parts and medicines.

Water is another important resource in British Columbia. Almost one-third of Canada's fresh water is in this province. Waterpower is used to make **electricity** at **hydro-electric plants**.

Agriculture and fishing, especially salmon fishing, are important to the province's economy.

British Columbia's dairy cattle make much of Canada's dairy products. These include milk, cheese, butter, and ice cream.

The province's most valuable resources are coal, **petroleum**, and **natural gas**. These are fuels. Fuels are mainly used to make heat and run motors. In the city of Burnaby is an oil refinery. This is where petroleum is made into lighter fuels. These fuels include gasoline, kerosene, diesel fuel, and jet fuel.

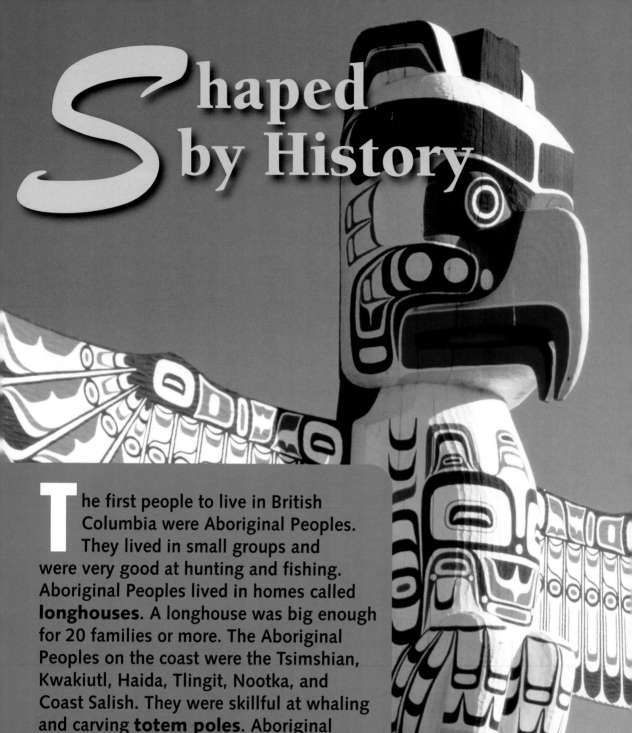

Shaped by History

The first people to live in British Columbia were Aboriginal Peoples. They lived in small groups and were very good at hunting and fishing. Aboriginal Peoples lived in homes called **longhouses**. A longhouse was big enough for 20 families or more. The Aboriginal Peoples on the coast were the Tsimshian, Kwakiutl, Haida, Tlingit, Nootka, and Coast Salish. They were skillful at whaling and carving **totem poles**. Aboriginal peoples of the mainland included the Interior Salish, the Athabaskans, and the Kootenay. They travelled from place to place following the animals they hunted. The lives of the Aboriginal Peoples changed in the 1700s when Europeans arrived.

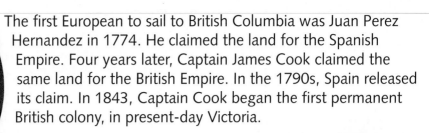

The first European to sail to British Columbia was Juan Perez Hernandez in 1774. He claimed the land for the Spanish Empire. Four years later, Captain James Cook claimed the same land for the British Empire. In the 1790s, Spain released its claim. In 1843, Captain Cook began the first permanent British colony, in present-day Victoria.

In 1793, a fur-trader named Sir Alexander Mackenzie was the first European to reach British Columbia from the East. He and other fur traders set up **trading posts** along the coast and on the main river routes. Some of these early posts grew into settlements, communities, and cities.

Gold was found in the Lower Fraser Valley in 1857. Thousands of people rushed to the area in search of gold. To help bring law and order to the area, the British government built the colony of British Columbia. James Douglas was made governor. In 1866, the gold rush ended.

In 1871, the colony of British Columbia joined with other British colonies to make one large dominion. This act was called Confederation. The Canadian Pacific Railway helped connect British Columbia to the rest of Canada. Settlers from other parts of Canada and from Great Britain used the train to move to British Columbia. They found jobs in lumber production, mining, and farming.

Art and Culture

British Columbia is home to 197 First Nations groups. They share their traditions through cultural displays. The world's largest collection of arts and crafts of the Pacific Northwest Aboriginal Peoples is shown at the Queen Charlotte Islands Museum in Skidegate. The museum has a rebuilt Haida village for visitors to explore.

Like Aboriginal Peoples, **immigrants** are an important part of British Columbia's heritage. Many British Columbians have ancestors from Europe and other parts of the world. They share their culture with others.

One of Canada's well-known artists, Emily Carr, was from British Columbia. Her paintings focus on the province's Aboriginal Peoples and its rain forests.

Film production and theatre are major art forms in British Columbia. Many feature films are made in Vancouver. Los Angeles and New York are the only other places in North America where more films are made. The Arts Club Theatre, in Victoria, is the largest regional theatre in western Canada.

In the late 1800s, thousands of people came to British Columbia from China. They helped build the Canadian Pacific Railway. Today, more than 100,000 British Columbians are related to these people. As in China, these British Columbians celebrate Chinese New Year with colourful street parades and giant dragons.

The culture of India is part of British Columbia. There are large Sikh settlements in Surrey and other places. Each year, the province's Hindu and Sikh communities enjoy fireworks to celebrate Diwali. This is a festival of lights that celebrates the victory of good over evil.

Points of Interest

British Columbia has many places to see and fun activities to enjoy. There are more than 850 provincial parks and protected areas in the province. Each year, about 15 million tourists visit its natural parks. Many provincial parks are in the region of the Rocky Mountains. Other attractions include the beaches, islands, and forests. There are many hiking trails and wildlife reserves. There are other activities, such as whale watching and fishing.

One of Vancouver's attractions is Stanley Park. This is one of the largest parks in North America. The park is surrounded on three sides by water. People come to this park to enjoy its towering trees, gardens, aquarium, tennis courts, and pitch-and-putt-golf course.

Strathcona Provincial Park is near the centre of Vancouver Island. It is home to a group of mountain peaks and hundreds of glaciers. These glaciers attract rock climbers and hikers. The most visited glacier is the Comox glacier. Hiking the entire Comox glacier takes three days.

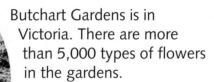

Butchart Gardens is in Victoria. There are more than 5,000 types of flowers in the gardens.

The Queen Charlotte Islands are found off the coast of British Columbia. Large parts of this area have been set-aside as parkland. People fly float planes to visit the islands from the mainland. On the islands, they enjoy hiking, kayaking, boating, and biking. They can visit the islands' towns and communities.

Sports and Activities

Many sports and activities
are played in British
Columbia. The province
was chosen to host the 2010
Winter Olympic and Paralympic
Games. They will take place in
Vancouver and Whistler. This event
will feature sports, such as alpine
skiing, ice hockey, bobsledding,
and speed skating. Other sports
enjoyed in British Columbia
include football, golfing, curling,
swimming, and kayaking.

The Vancouver Canucks play in the National Hockey League (NHL). They help raise money for children's health and wellness. The team's Canucks for Kids Fund has raised millions of dollars for children's charities. Their home arena is the General Motors Place in Vancouver.

In 2006, British Columbia hosted many sporting events. These included the Curling Canada Cup, the Pan Pacific Swimming Championships, and the Canadian Legion Track and Field National Championships. The province also hosted the World Junior Hockey Championships and a track and field event called the World Athletics Masters Championships.

In 2007, British Columbia hosted the Union Cycliste Internationale BMX World Championships in Victoria. This event is a race of off-road (BMX) bicycles. The province also hosted a soccer tournament in both Victoria and Vancouver. This tournament is called the Fédération Internationale de Football Association (FIFA) Men's World Youth Championships 2007.

There are many places in British Columbia for whale watching. Whale watchers can ride on an ocean kayak, boat, or canoe. They may see a variety of whale species, including orca, humpback, and grey. The splash of an orca whale can be heard for many kilometres.

What Others Are Saying

Many people have great things to say about British Columbia.

"British Columbia can rightly boast of having a first-class park and protected area system. The province can proudly boast of having Canada's largest protected area system, second only to the country's national parks."

"B.C. is ready-made for exploring. The geography and adventures are so diverse that few other places in North America can offer the variety British Columbia can. It is an outdoor recreational haven."

"British Columbia has plenty to celebrate—and much more to look forward to…. It is the forest province in a forest nation, the greatest fish supplier in a land of fishermen, the source of as much potential hydro-electric power as ten St. Lawrence power projects."

"The Province of British Columbia may fitly be described as the California of Canada; and on account of its great natural resources it will, before long, become one of the most important places in the world."

ACTION Think about the place where you live. Come up with some words to describe your province, city, or community. Are there rolling hills and deep valleys? Can you see trees or lakes? What are some of the features of the land, people, and buildings that make your home special? Use these words to write a paragraph about the place where you live.

Test Your Knowledge

What have you learned about British Columbia? Try answering the following questions.

1 What two countries claimed to own the land of British Columbia before it became a colony? Visit the library, or use a computer to read more about the History of British Columbia. Learn how it became part of Canada and why other countries wanted the land.

2 When did British Columbia join Confederation? Research when the other provinces joined and why they wanted to become part of Canada.

4 What is the capital of British Columbia? Draw a map of British Columbia and show the location of its capital. Write a paragraph about some of the fun things to do in the capital. You can find more information online about the capital by visiting Kids' Stuff in British Columbia, at www.britishcolumbia.com/attractions/?id=30

3 If you could take a trip to British Columbia, what places would you like to see? What kinds of activities would you do? Would you need binoculars, a swimming suit, snow skis, or hiking shoes? What other items would you pack?

Be a Tour Guide

Imagine you are a tour guide in British Columbia. Write a plan for your tour. Include a list of the places you and your guests will visit. Write a short speech to welcome your guests to British Columbia.

Further Research

Books

To find out more about British Columbia and other Canadian provinces and territories, visit your local library. Most libraries have computers that connect to a database for researching information. If you input a key word, you will be provided with a list of books in the library that contain information on that topic. Non-fiction books are arranged numerically, using their call number. Fiction books are organized alphabetically by the author's last name.

Websites

The World Wide Web is a good source of information. Reliable websites usually include government sites, educational sites, and online encyclopedias. Visit the following sites to learn more about British Columbia.

Go to the Government of British Columbia's website to learn about the province's government, history, and climate.
www.gov.bc.ca/bvprd/bc/home.do

Visit CanadaInfoLink for everything you want to know about Canada and British Columbia. Learn facts about the Cariboo Gold Rush and rare wildlife. You can take a quiz on what you have learned.
www.canadainfolink.ca/bcmap.htm

Check out Kidzone, a website with photos of British Columbia, as well as worksheets and colouring pages.
www.kidzone.ws/geography/bc

Glossary

electricity: a form of energy produced by the movement of electrons

First Nations: members of Canada's Aboriginal community who are not Inuit or Métis

genetic trait: a physical feature, such as eye and hair colour

hydro-electric plants: places where powerful water drives a machine that makes electricity

immigrants: people who leave their homeland to move to another country

longhouses: long, narrow, single-room buildings

natural gas: a fossil fuel in the gaseous state used for cooking and heating homes

petroleum: a thick, dark oil found beneath Earth's surface that can be turned into gasoline, kerosene, and other products

softwood: wood products made from cone-bearing trees

totem poles: poles carved from trees by Aboriginal Peoples of the northwest coast to tell a story

trading posts: stores where people traded goods

Union Jack: the British flag

Index